AF588486

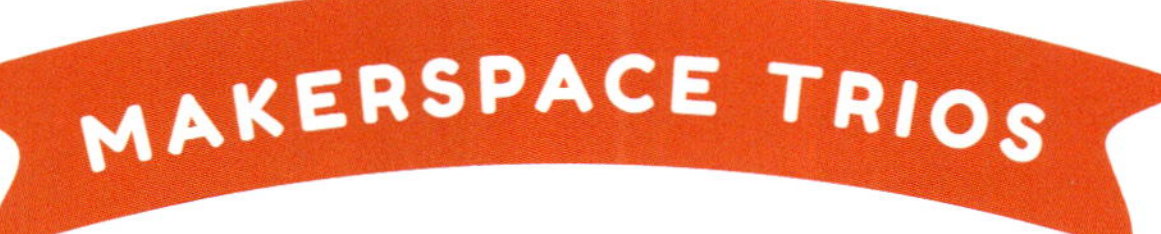

Creating with PAPER TUBES, RUBBER BANDS & YARN

Elsie Olson

Consulting Editor, Diane Craig,
M.A./Reading Specialist

Super Sandcastle

An Imprint of Abdo Publishing
abdobooks.com

abdobooks.com

Published by Abdo Publishing, a division of ABDO, PO Box 398166, Minneapolis, Minnesota 55439.

Printed in the United States of America, North Mankato, Minnesota
102021
012022

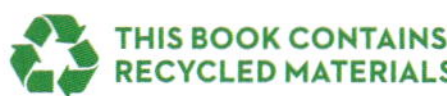

Design: Sarah DeYoung, Mighty Media, Inc.
Production: Mighty Media, Inc.
Editor: Megan Borgert-Spaniol
Cover Photographs: iStockphoto; Mighty Media, Inc.; Shutterstock Images
Interior Photographs: Anastassia Elias/Flickr; Andrew Milligan/AP Images; erika g./Flickr; Groove Press/Flickr; iStockphoto; Martin Stær Andersen/Flickr; Mighty Media, Inc.; Shutterstock Images

The following manufacturers/names appearing in this book are trademarks: ArtMinds™, Elmer's®

Library of Congress Control Number: 2021944395

Publisher's Cataloging-in-Publication Data
Names: Olson, Elsie, author.
Title: Creating with paper tubes, rubber bands & yarn / by Elsie Olson
Description: Minneapolis, Minnesota : Abdo Publishing, 2022 | Series: Makerspace trios | Includes online resources and index.
Identifiers: ISBN 9781532196454 (lib. bdg.) | ISBN 9781098218263 (ebook)
Subjects: LCSH: Handicraft--Juvenile literature. | Creative thinking--Juvenile literature. | Cardboard tube craft--Juvenile literature. | Rubber band craft--Juvenile literature. | Yarn in art--Juvenile literature. | Mixed media crafts--Juvenile literature.
Classification: DDC 745.5--dc23

Super SandCastle™ books are created by a team of professional educators, reading specialists, and content developers around five essential components—phonemic awareness, phonics, vocabulary, text comprehension, and fluency—to assist young readers as they develop reading skills and strategies and increase their general knowledge. All books are written, reviewed, and leveled for guided reading and early reading intervention programs for use in shared, guided, and independent reading and writing activities to support a balanced approach to literacy instruction.

TO ADULT HELPERS

The projects in this book are fun and simple. There are just a few things to remember to keep kids safe. Some projects may use sharp or hot objects. Also, kids may be using messy supplies. Make sure they protect their clothes and work surfaces. Be ready to offer guidance during brainstorming and assist when necessary.

CONTENTS

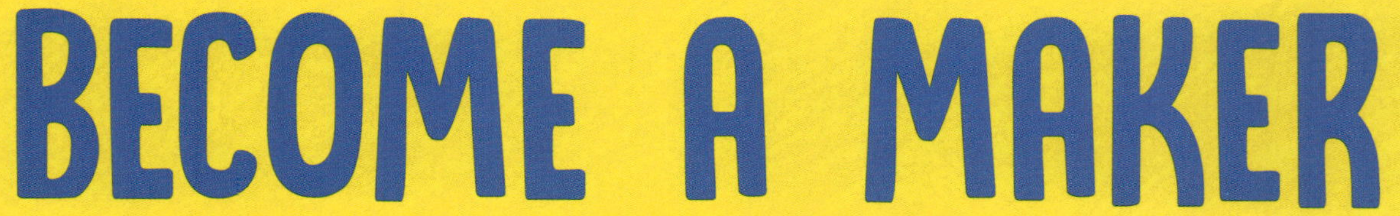

A makerspace is like a laboratory. It's a place where ideas are formed and problems are solved. Kids like you create amazing things in makerspaces. Many makerspaces are in schools and libraries. But they can also be in kitchens, bedrooms, and backyards. Anywhere can be a makerspace when you use imagination, inspiration, **collaboration**, and problem-solving!

Makerspace Toolbox

Imagination

This takes you to new places and lets you experience new things. Anything is possible with imagination!

Inspiration

This is the spark that gives you an idea. Inspiration can come from almost anywhere!

Collaboration

Makers work together. They ask questions and get ideas from everyone around them. Collaboration solves problems that seem impossible.

Problem-Solving

Things often don't go as planned when you're creating. But that's part of the fun! Find creative solutions to any problem that comes up. These will make your project even better.

EXPLORE PAPER TUBES

You probably come across paper tubes nearly every day. These hollow tubes are made from cardboard. They can be used to store rolls of paper, like toilet paper, paper towels, or wrapping paper.

Paper Tube Properties

- Hollow
- Lightweight
- Stiff
- Sturdy

How Can You Use Paper Tubes?

Paper tubes usually store paper products. But they can be used however you like in a makerspace! Let your imagination wander. What would it look like to use paper tubes in a new way?

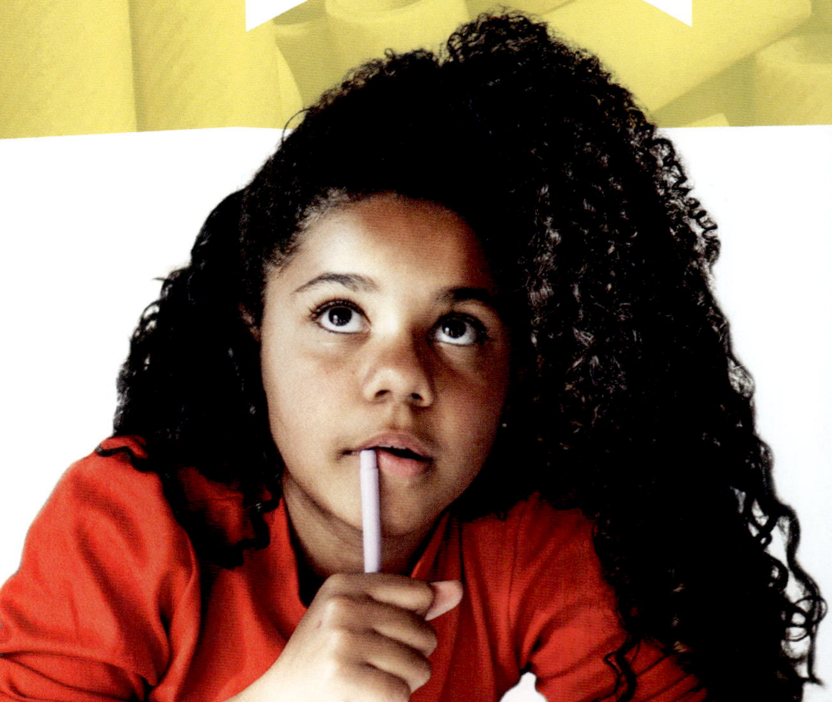

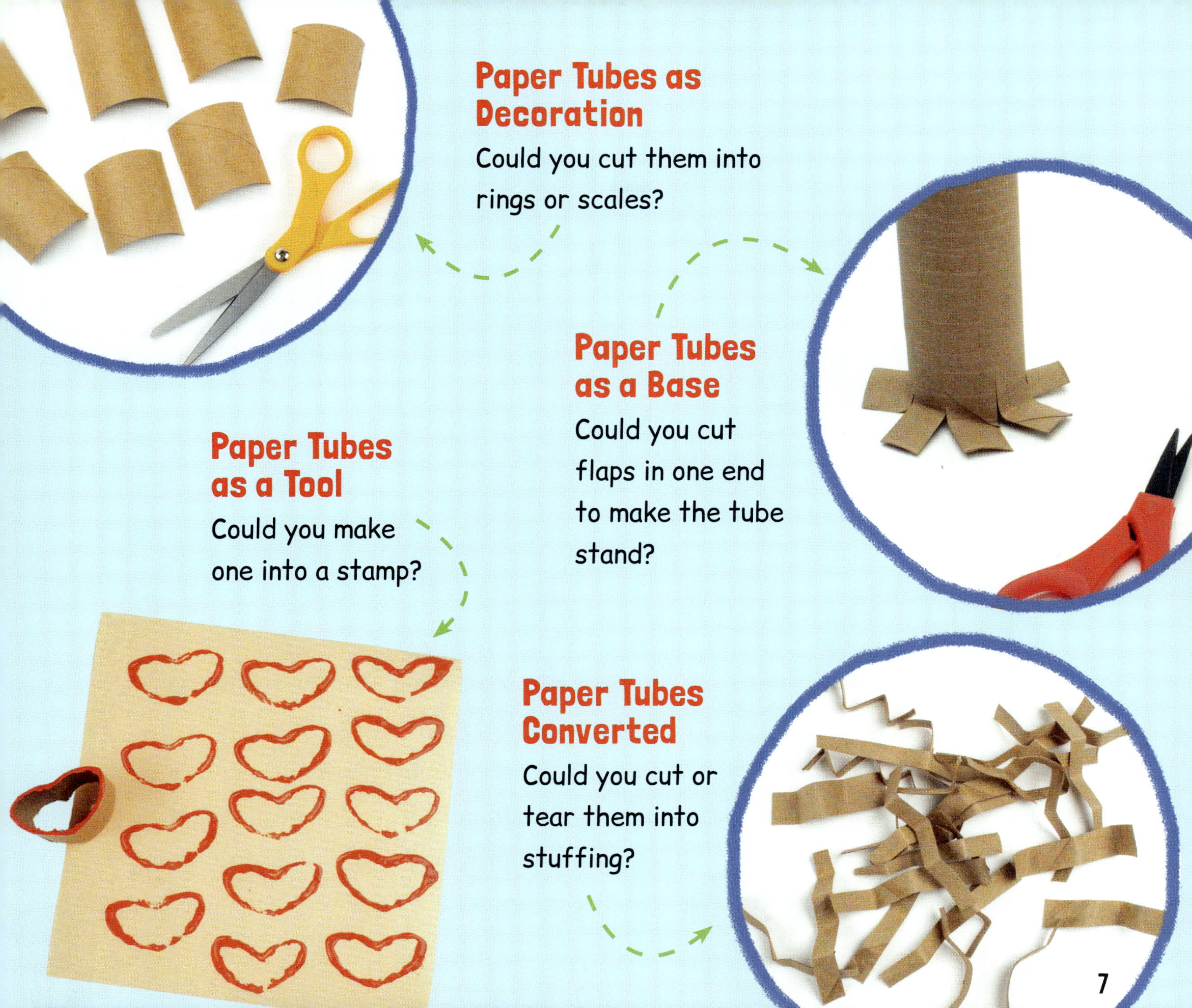

Paper Tubes as Decoration

Could you cut them into rings or scales?

Paper Tubes as a Base

Could you cut flaps in one end to make the tube stand?

Paper Tubes as a Tool

Could you make one into a stamp?

Paper Tubes Converted

Could you cut or tear them into stuffing?

EXPLORE RUBBER BANDS

Rubber bands are common tools. They are often used to hold things together, such as bunches of vegetables and rolled-up paper. Rubber bands can also help close bags, open jars, and much more!

Rubber Band Properties

- Circular
- Flexible
- Rubbery
- Stretchy

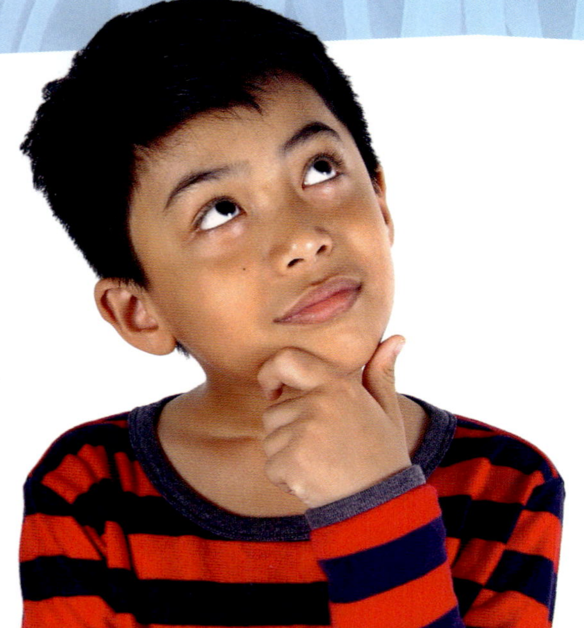

How Can You Use Rubber Bands?

Rubber bands have many standard uses. But they can be used however you like in a makerspace! Let your imagination wander. What would it look like to use rubber bands in a new way?

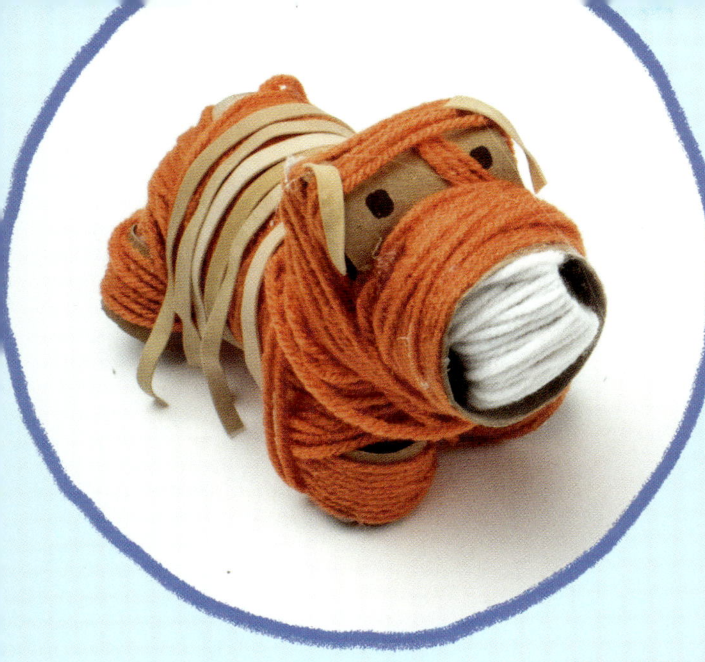

Rubber Bands as Decoration

Could you cut them into hair?

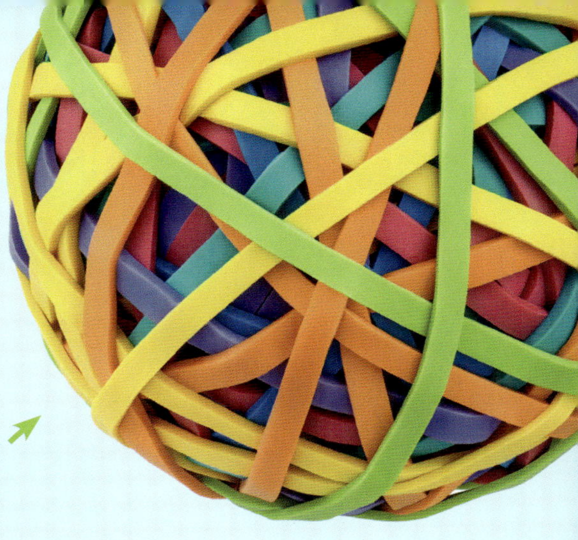

Rubber Bands as a Base

Could you wrap many of them into a ball?

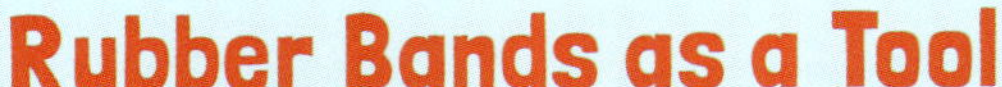

Rubber Bands as a Tool

Could you use one as a hanger?

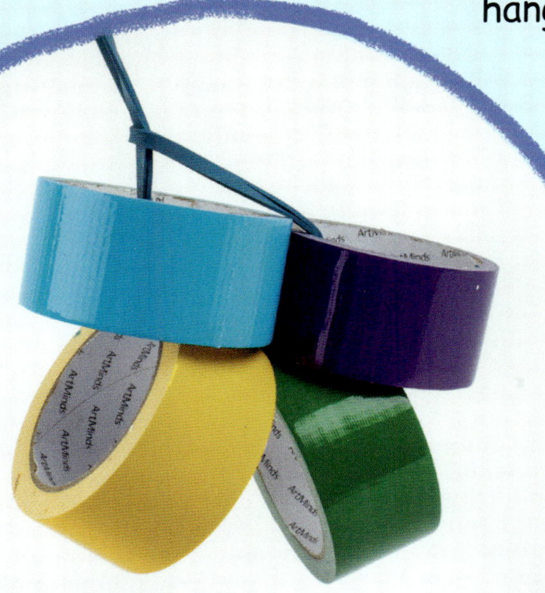

Rubber Bands Converted

Could you loop them into a long chain?

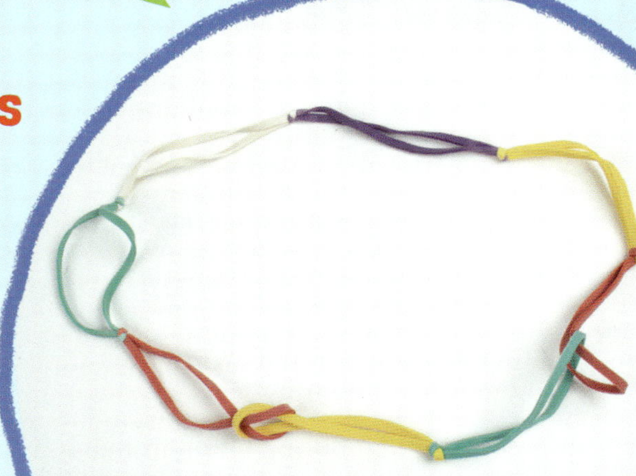

EXPLORE YARN

Yarn is made of many fibers twisted together. Yarn can be dyed all kinds of different colors. It is then used to make clothing items, such as hats, sweaters, and mittens.

Yarn Properties

- Colorful
- Flexible
- Long
- Soft

How Can You Use Yarn?

Yarn is often used for knitting. But it can be used however you like in a makerspace! Let your imagination wander. What would it look like to use yarn in a new way?

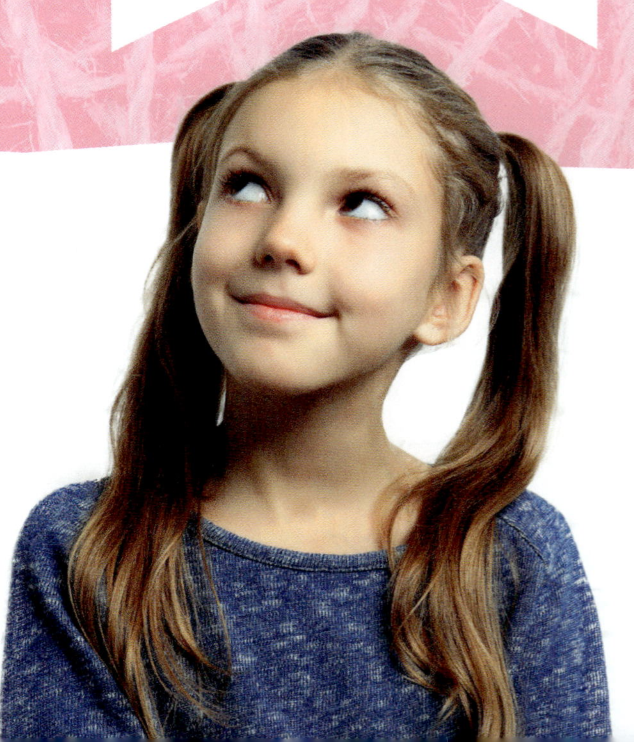

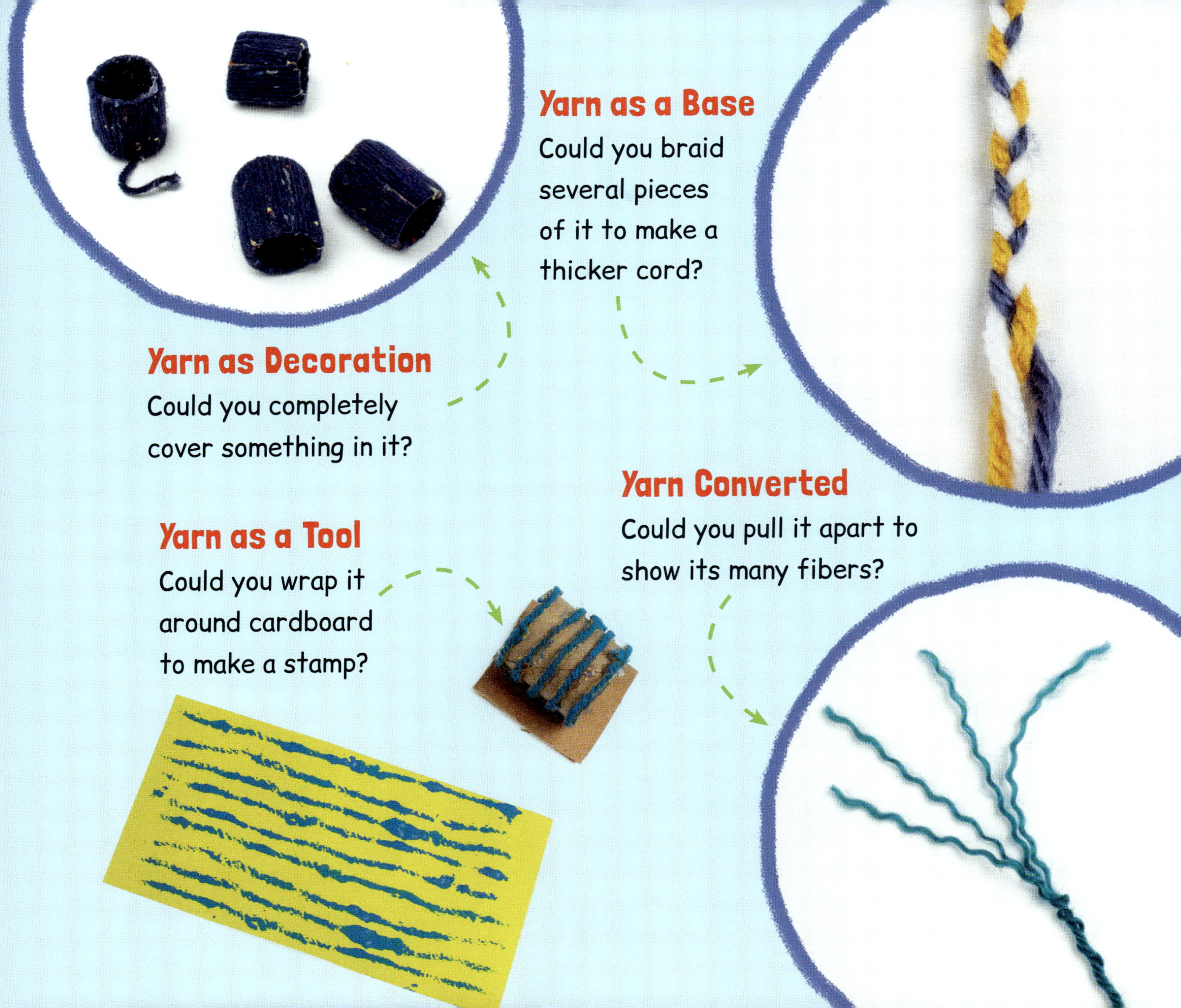

Yarn as a Base

Could you braid several pieces of it to make a thicker cord?

Yarn as Decoration

Could you completely cover something in it?

Yarn Converted

Could you pull it apart to show its many fibers?

Yarn as a Tool

Could you wrap it around cardboard to make a stamp?

GET INSPIRED

People have used paper tubes, rubber bands, and yarn in all kinds of creative ways. Let these examples spark your imagination!

Artist Anastassia Elias creates tiny paper scenes inside paper tubes.

A wall hanging made of recycled paper tubes

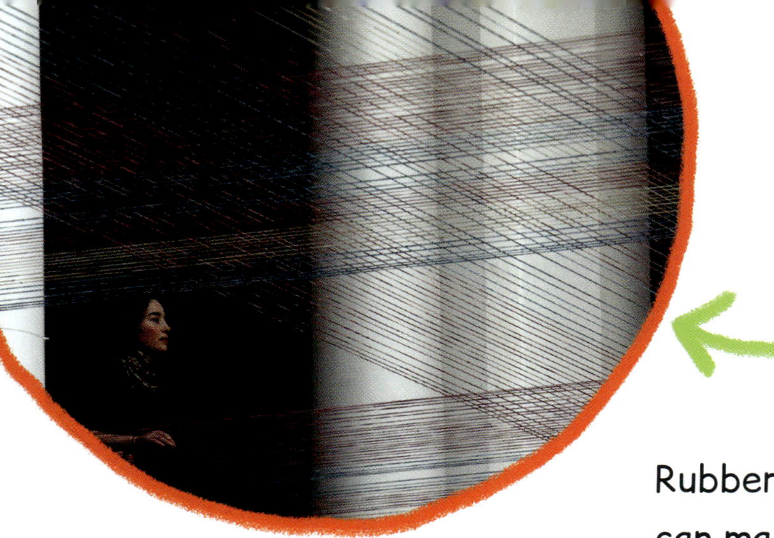

In 2009, artist Daniela Justiniano created a rubber band display in Edinburgh, Scotland. She used more than 25,000 rubber bands!

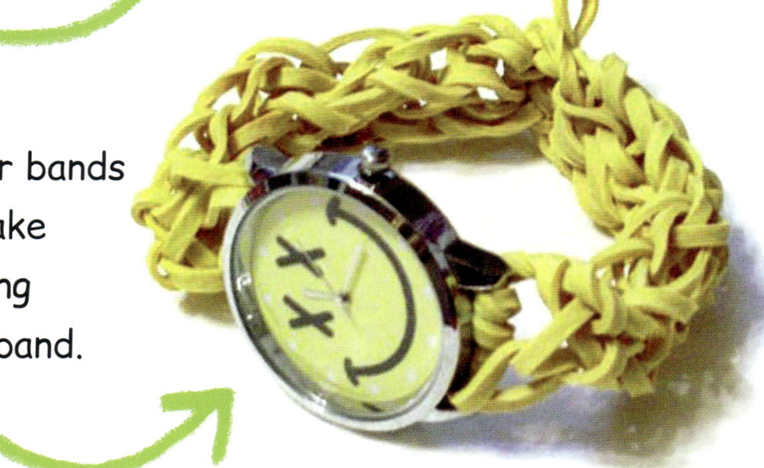

Rubber bands can make a strong watchband.

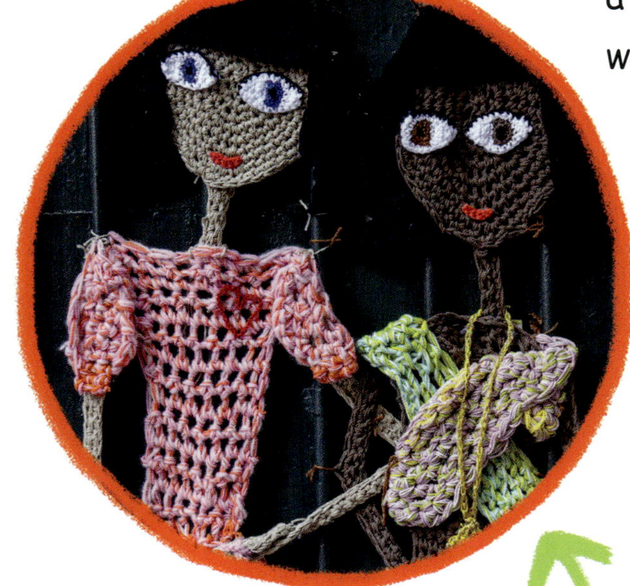

Yarn street art in Milan, Italy

Artist Magda Sayeg uses yarn to brighten public spaces, such as these stairs in Sydney, Australia.

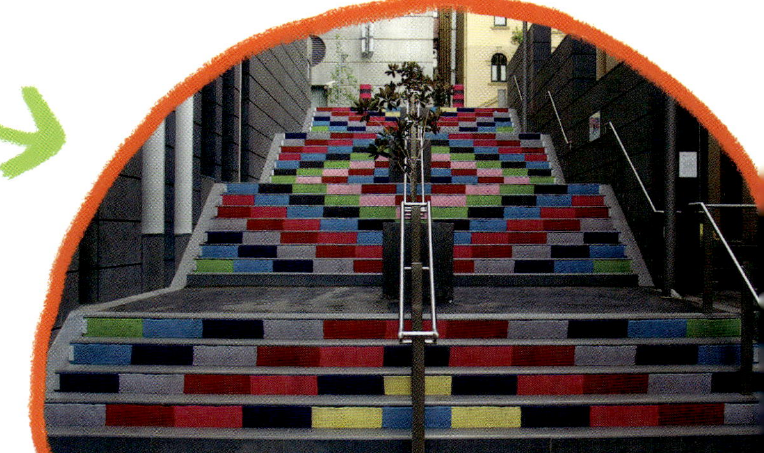

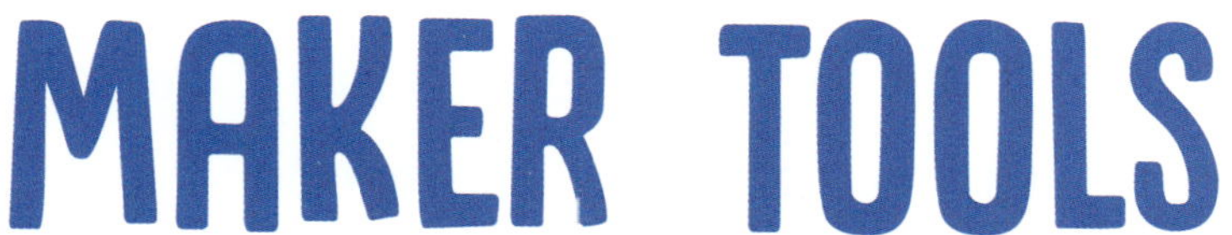

MAKER TOOLS

Are you inspired? Have you brainstormed some makerspace projects? It's time to gather your paper tubes, rubber bands, and yarn. You may also need a few everyday tools to cut and connect your primary materials.

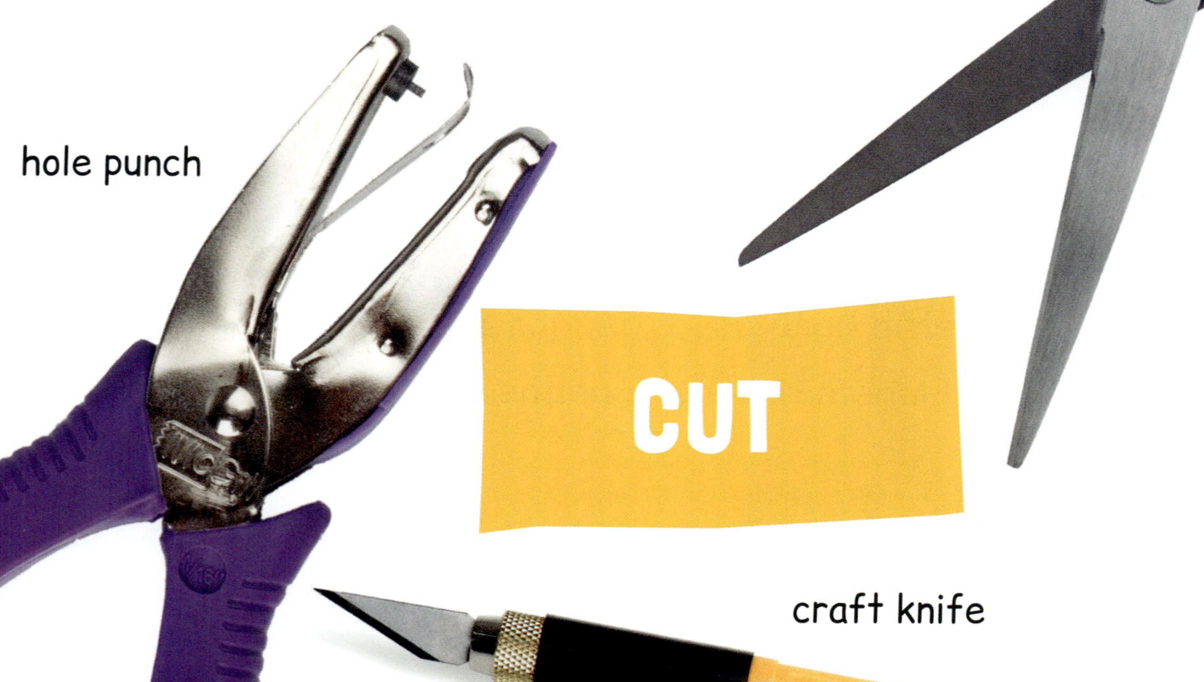

scissors

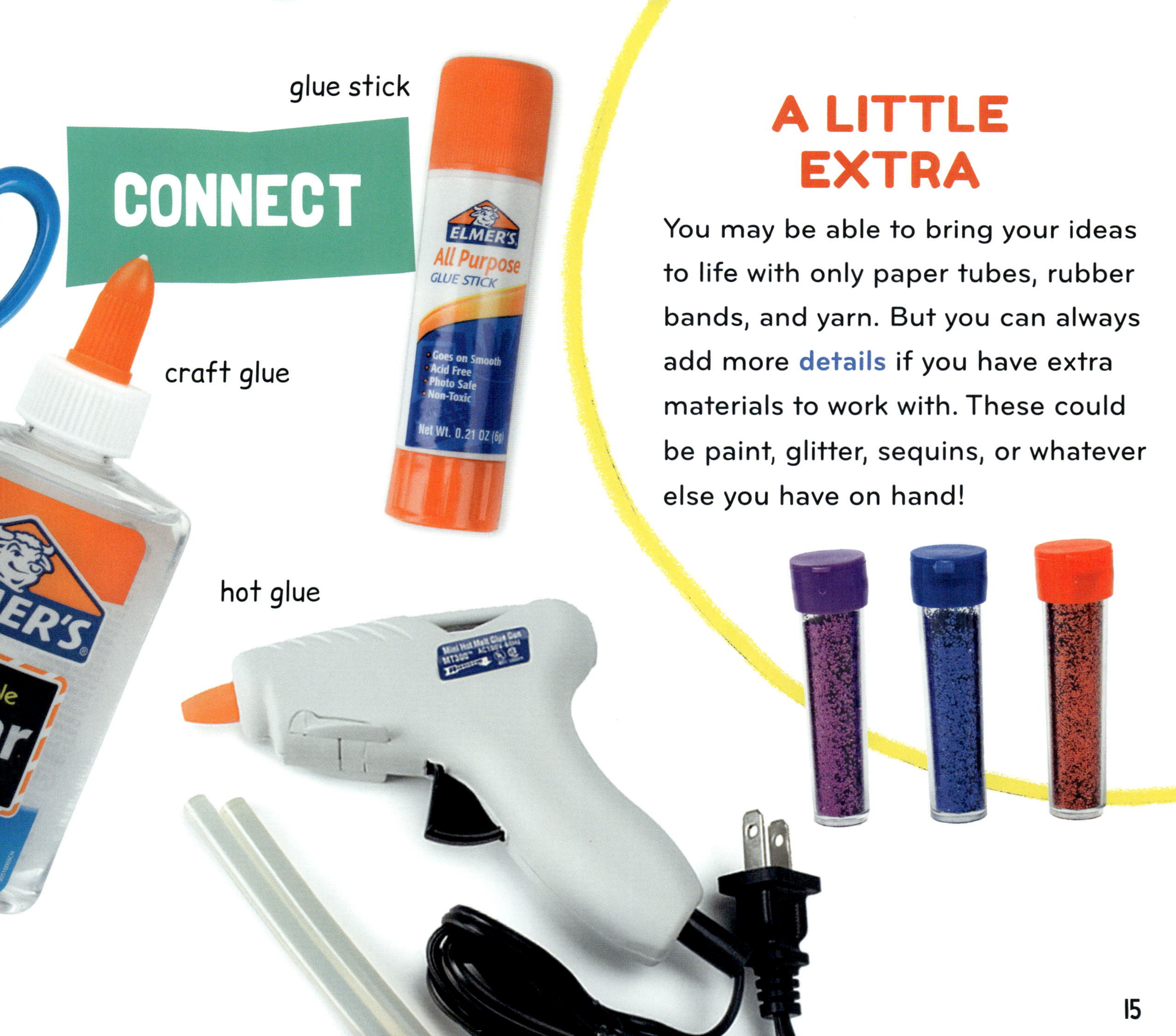

A LITTLE EXTRA

You may be able to bring your ideas to life with only paper tubes, rubber bands, and yarn. But you can always add more **details** if you have extra materials to work with. These could be paint, glitter, sequins, or whatever else you have on hand!

MAKING YOUR MAKERSPACE

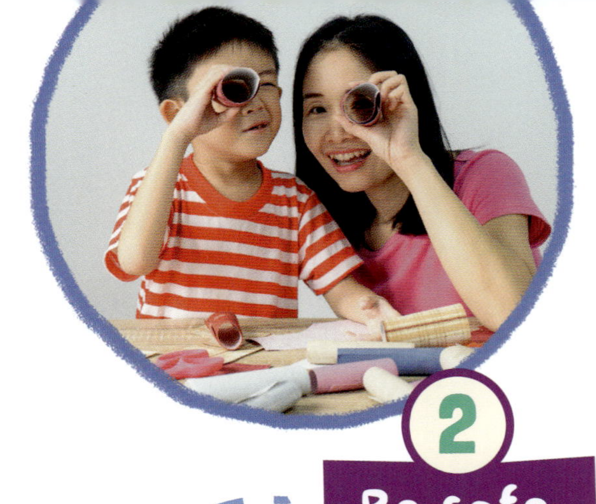

You can let your imagination run wild in a makerspace. But be sure to follow these rules to stay safe and be respectful.

1

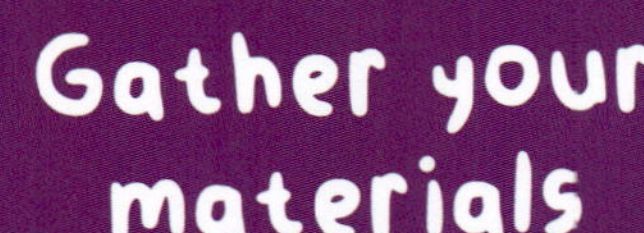

Gather your materials

Make sure an adult says it's OK to use what you gather.

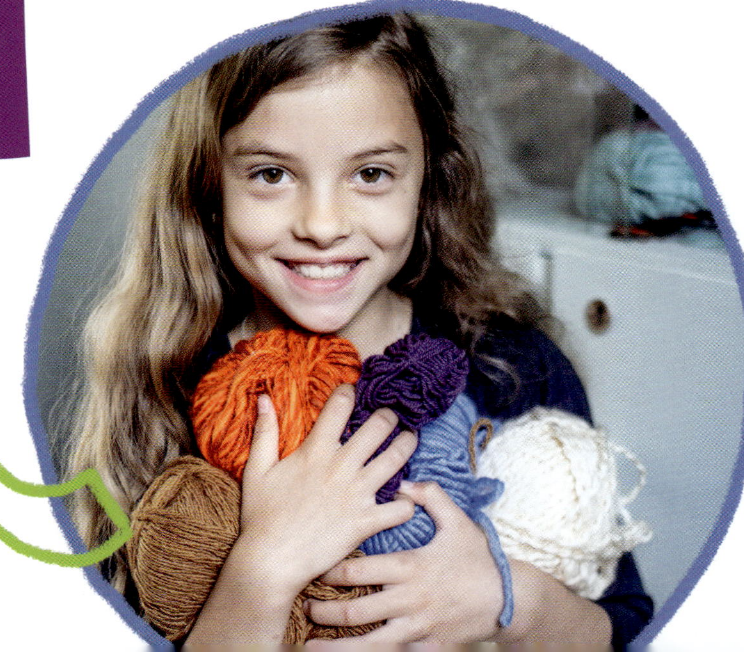

2

Be safe

Ask an adult for help when using sharp or hot tools, such as craft knives or glue guns.

Share the space

Share supplies and space with other makers. You can invite them to share their ideas if you're feeling stuck!

Keep trying

Don't give up when things don't go exactly as planned. Instead, think about the problem you are having. What are some ways to solve it?

Clean up

Put away materials. Find a safe space to store unfinished projects until next time. And clean up any scraps, spills, or messes you made.

DISPLAY IT

Create an artwork from paper tubes, rubber bands, and yarn. Then put it on display!

Cut paper tubes in half the long way. Glue them together to create a **3D canvas**.

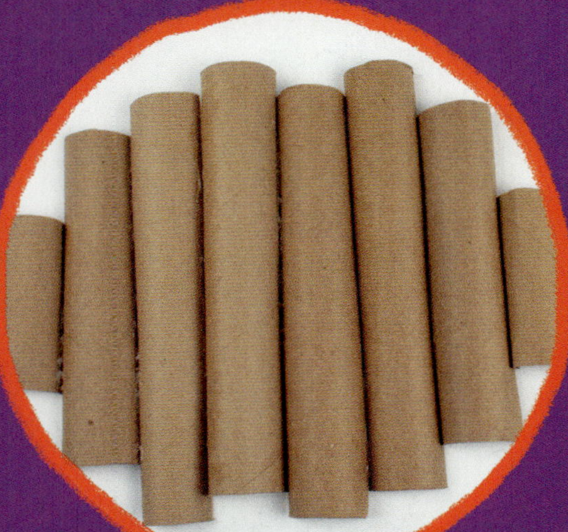

Glue pieces of yarn and rubber band to make a scene on your canvas.

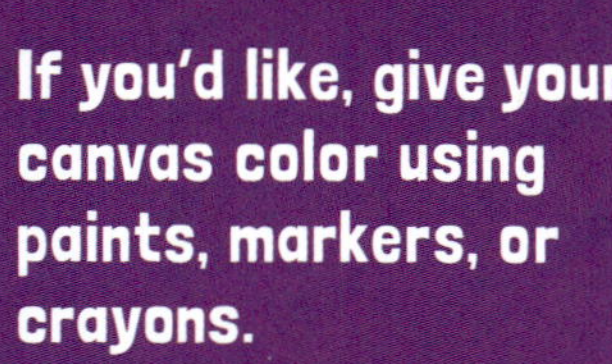

If you'd like, give your canvas color using paints, markers, or crayons.

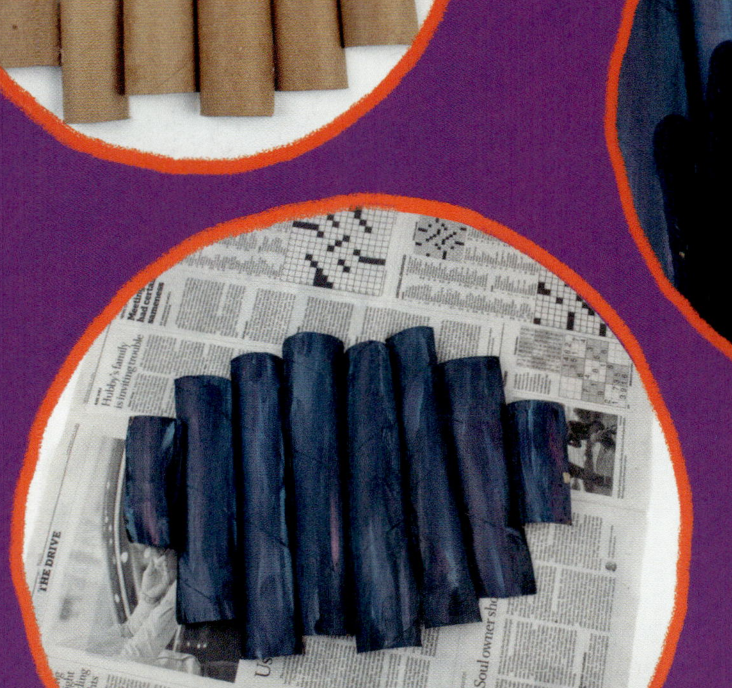

Make a cord of braided yarn to hang your artwork!

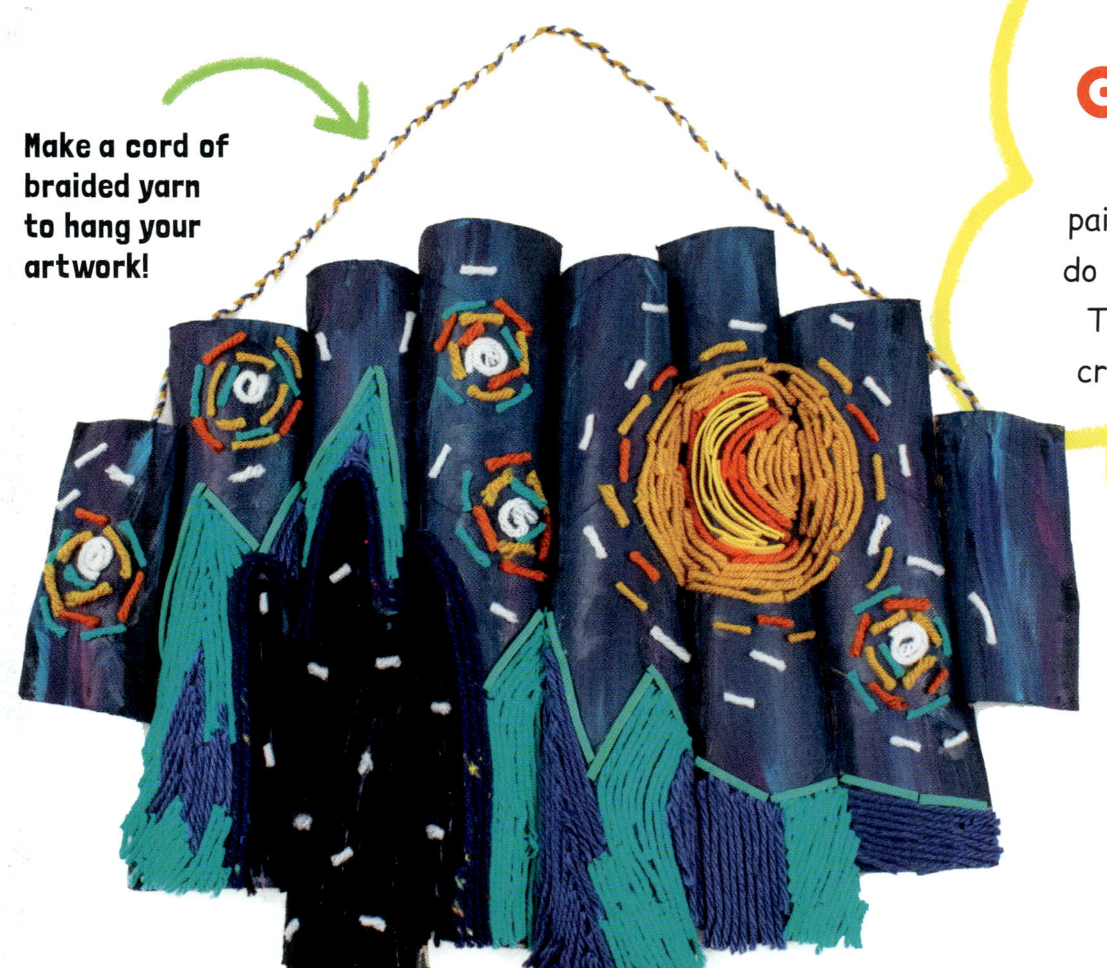

Get Inspired

What kinds of statues, paintings, and other artworks do you see in your community? Think about how they were created as you come up with your own designs.

Your Turn!

Could you create a life-size statue out of paper towel or wrapping paper tubes?

What kind of scene could you create out of large, medium, and mini rubber bands?

What existing object could you turn into art by wrapping it in yarn?

WEAR IT

What wearable clothing or accessories could you make from paper tubes, rubber bands, and yarn?

Cut paper tubes in half the long way and flatten the halves. Glue them together to make a crown.

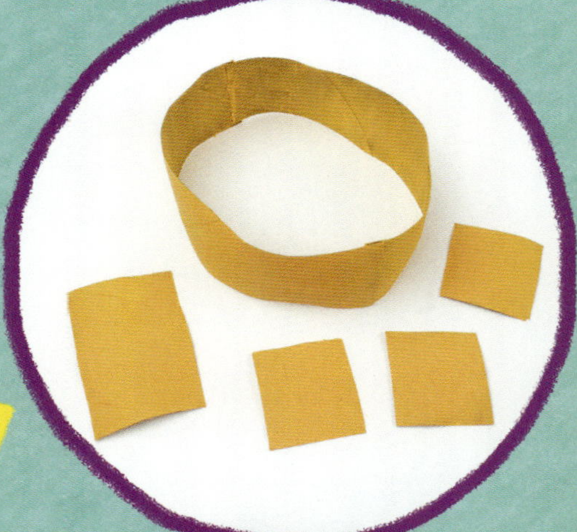

Tie together pieces of yarn to make pom-poms. Tie the pom-poms to your crown spikes.

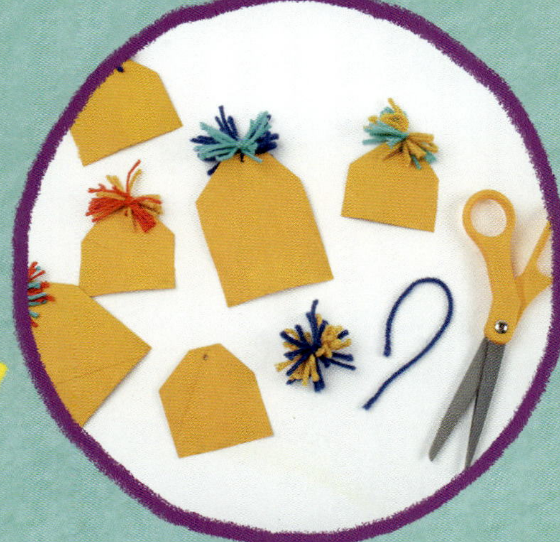

Cut up rubber bands to make confetti to decorate your crown.

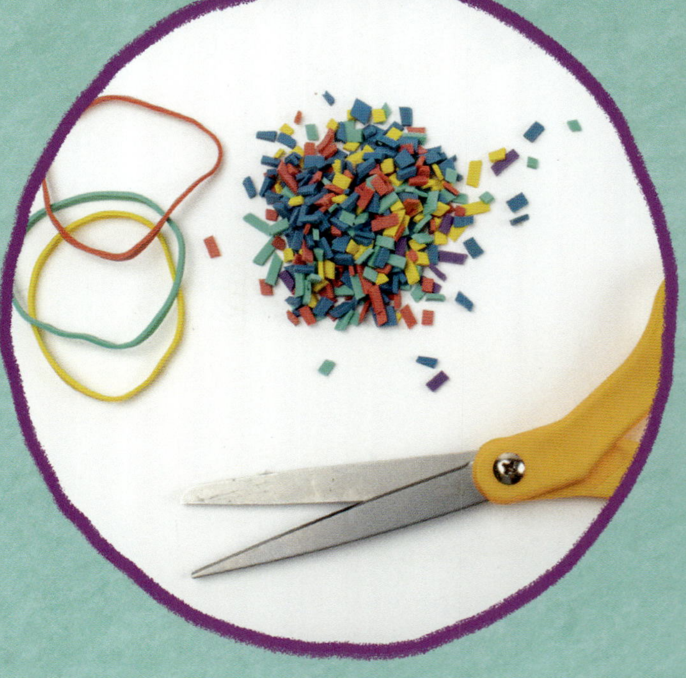

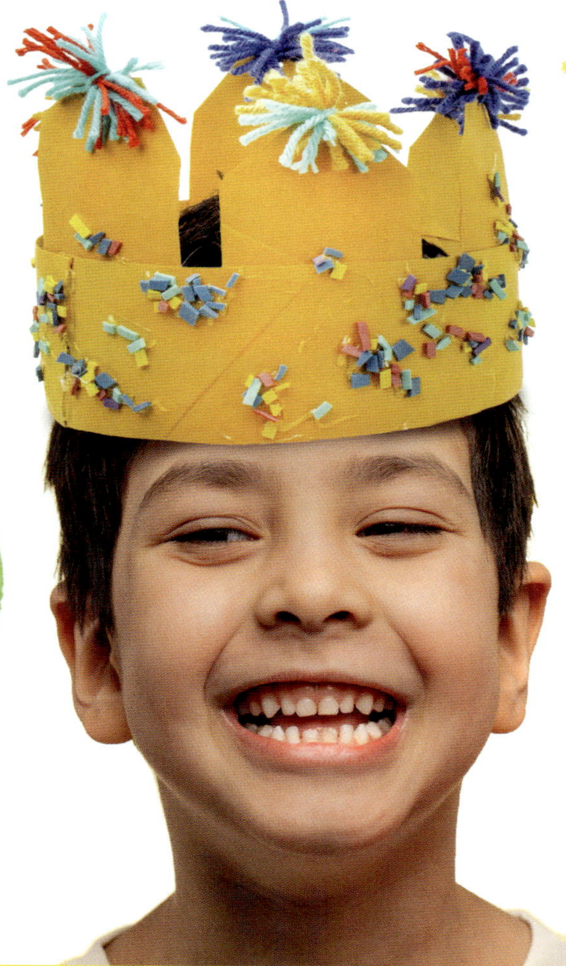

Collaborate

Don't be afraid to ask a friend or classmate for help with your project. Other makers might have ideas you didn't think of! They can also lend a hand during construction.

Wear your party crown on your birthday, a holiday, or any other special day!

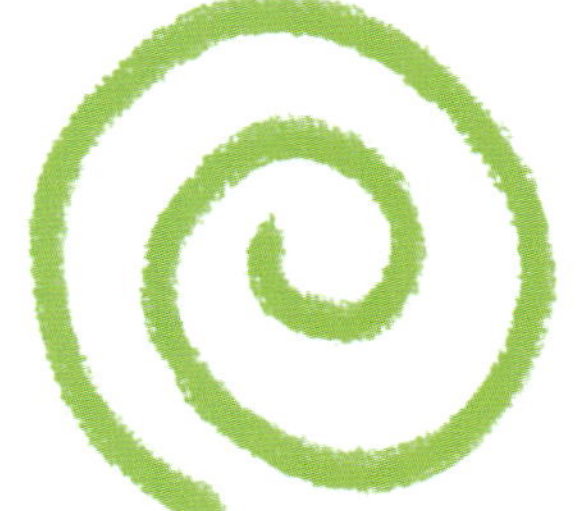

Your Turn!

How would you turn a paper tube into a bracelet or wrist cuff?

How could you use rubber bands to make a no-slip grip for your shoes?

Could you loop and tie pieces of yarn to make a belt or **suspenders**?

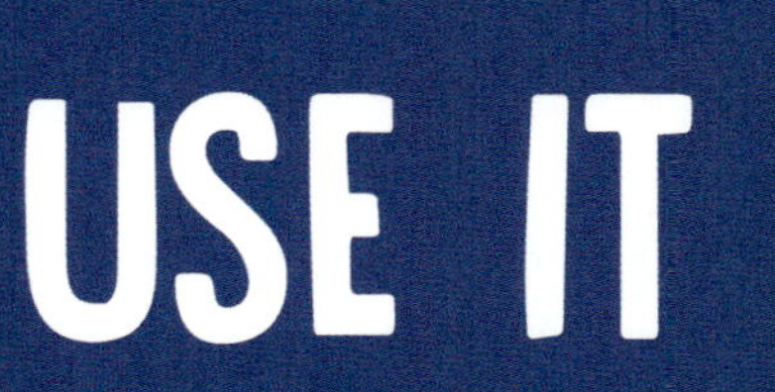

Think of an item you need. Then **design** it! Paper tubes, rubber bands, and yarn provide many options for functional projects.

Cut four flaps in one end of a paper tube. Fold the flaps together to close the tube.

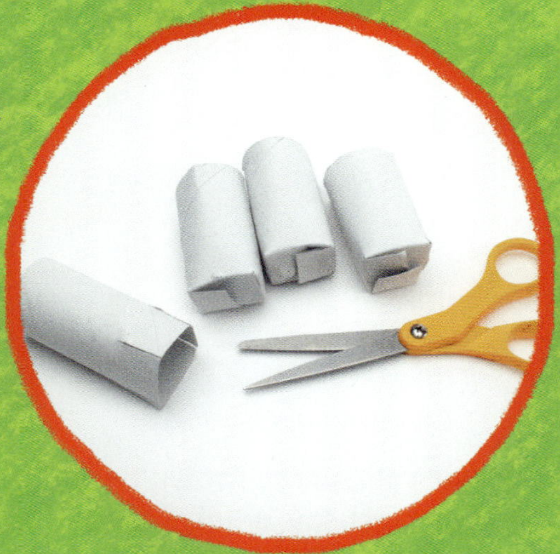

Use rubber bands to connect several yarn-wrapped tubes.

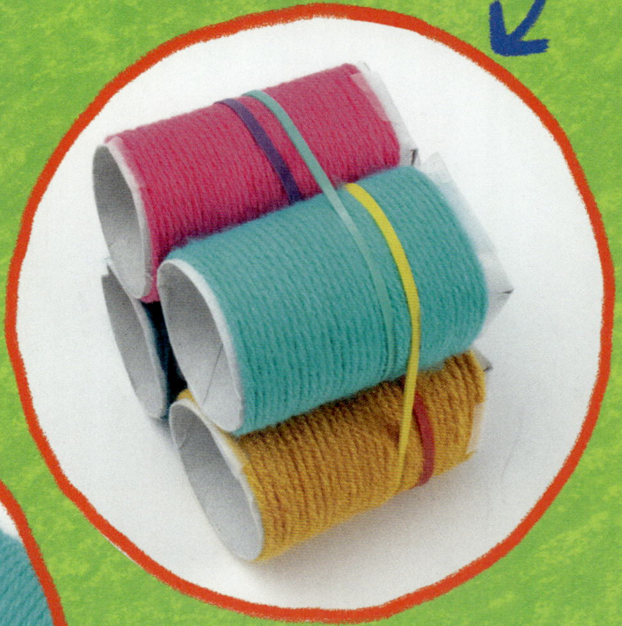

Wrap the tubes in yarn for a bit of color.

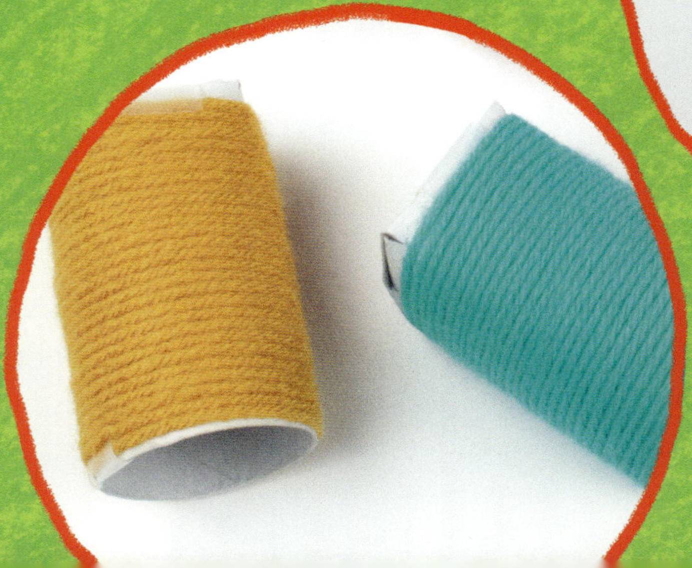

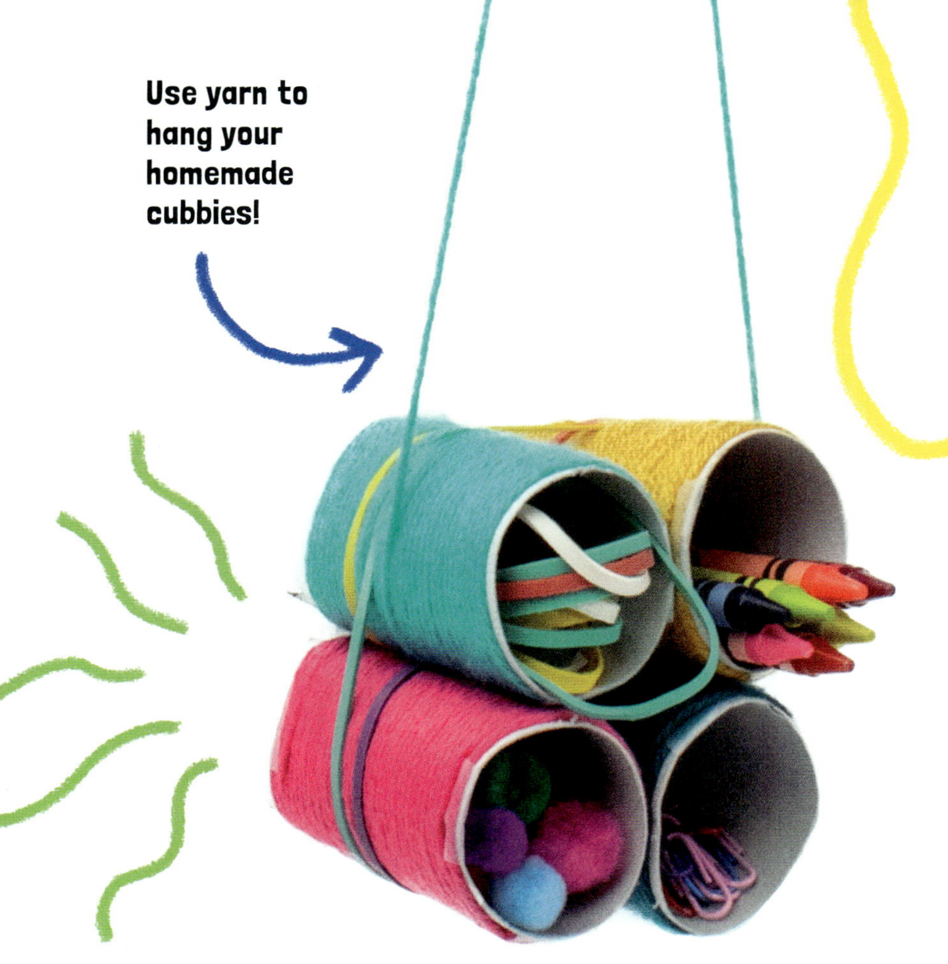

Imagine

Imagine ideas outside your own space and time. What sort of object might have been useful for people who lived in ancient Egypt?

Your Turn!

Could wrapping paper tubes be turned into a telescope?

Could you stretch rubber bands into a **grid** to organize pens and pencils?

How would you weave yarn into a water bottle carrier?

BUILD IT

Engineers use all kinds of materials to build. What do you want to construct? Can you do it using only paper tubes, rubber bands, and yarn?

Cut flaps in one end of a paper towel tube. Fold them out to make a tower base. Wrap the tower in yarn to add some color and make it sturdier.

Poke two holes in the top of each tower. Tie the ends of the bridge cables through the holes.

Cut a wide rubber band to make two main cables. Connect the main cables with smaller rubber bands to make a bridge deck.

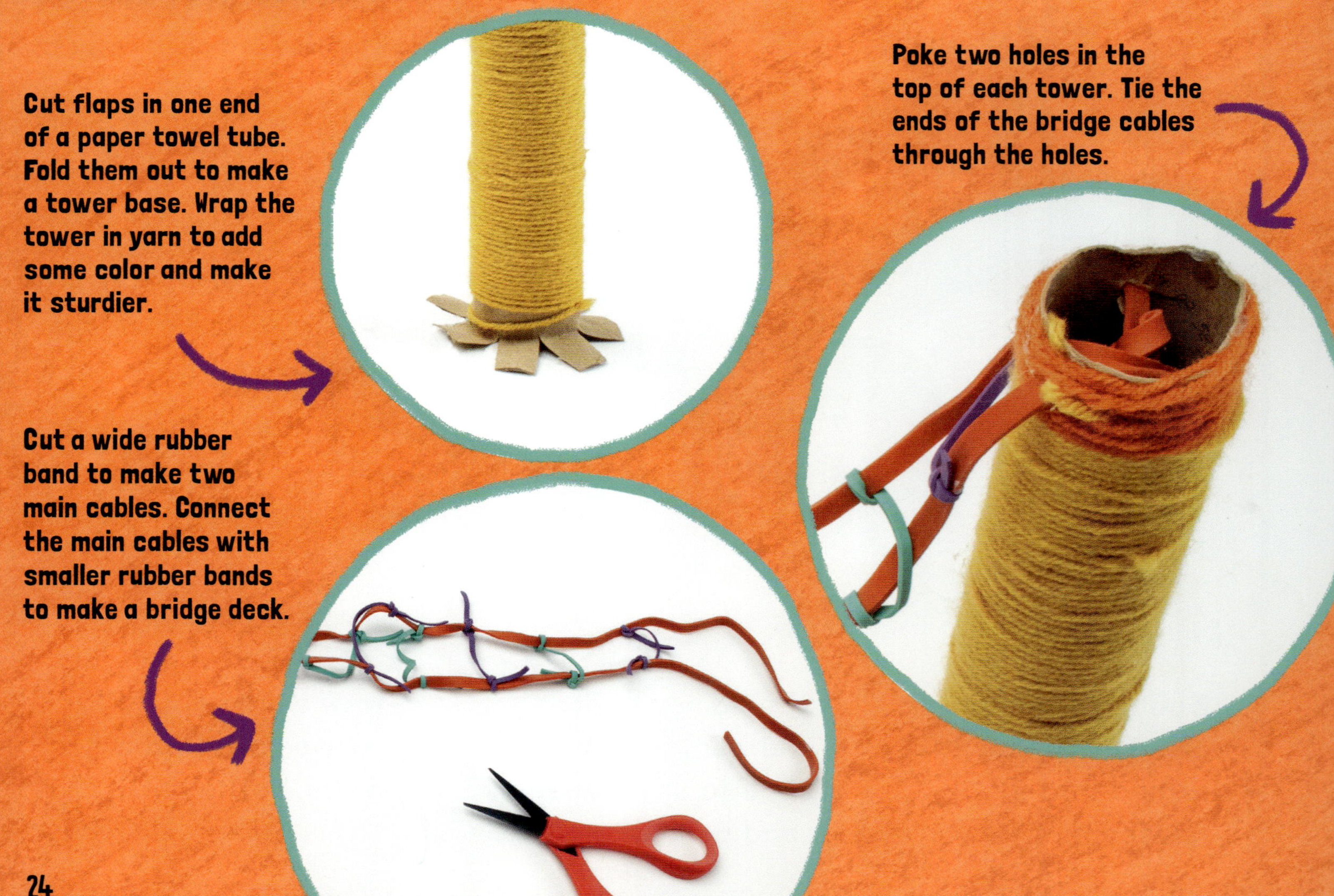

Problem-Solve

Every problem has more than one solution. Is your bridge tipping over? Try giving the towers wider bases or extra supports. You could also lower the bridge deck so it is closer to the ground.

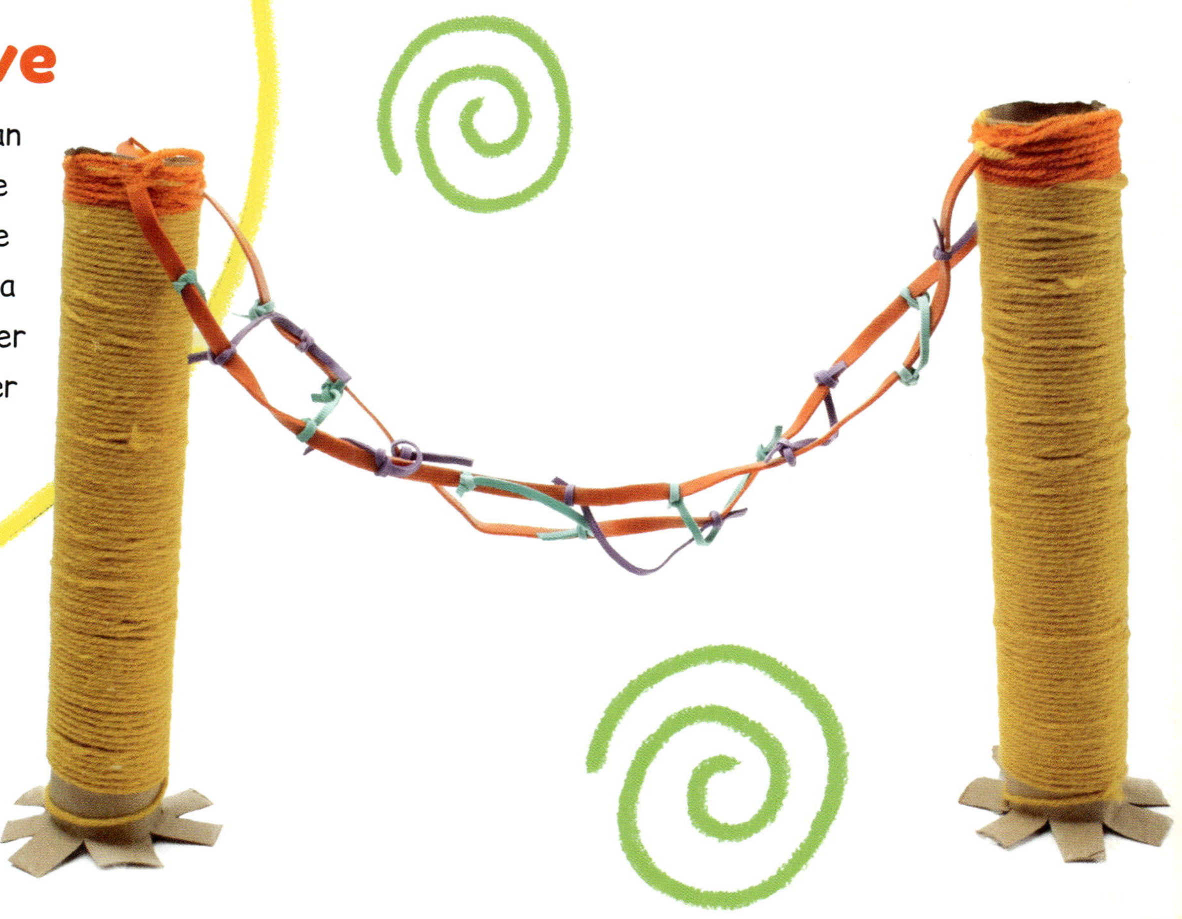

Your Turn!

How would you turn a paper tube into a rocket?

Could you build a fishing net out of rubber bands?

How would you build a tent out of yarn?

GIFT IT

Is a holiday or birthday coming up? Do you want to surprise a friend or family member just for fun? You can make all kinds of homemade gifts using paper tubes, rubber bands, and yarn.

Combine different lengths of paper tubes to make an animal shape.

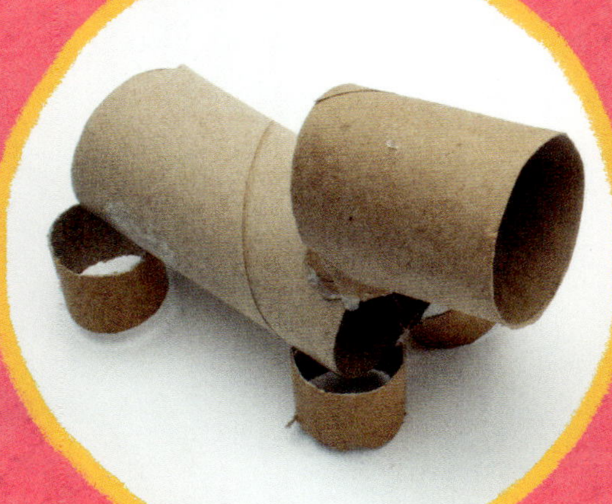

Wrap your creature in yarn to make a fur coat.

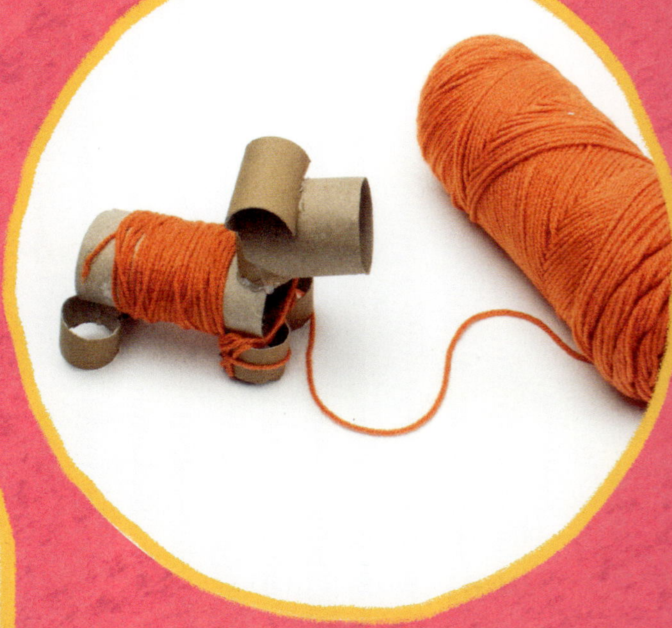

Use the curve of a paper tube to create features such as horns or a nose.

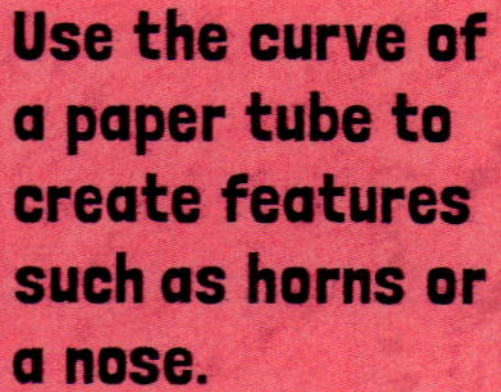

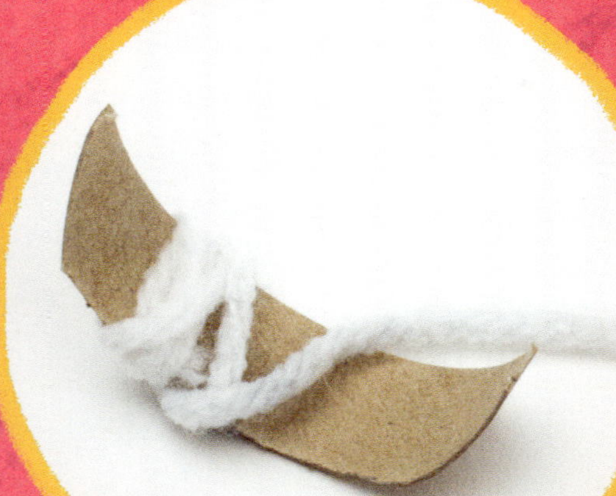

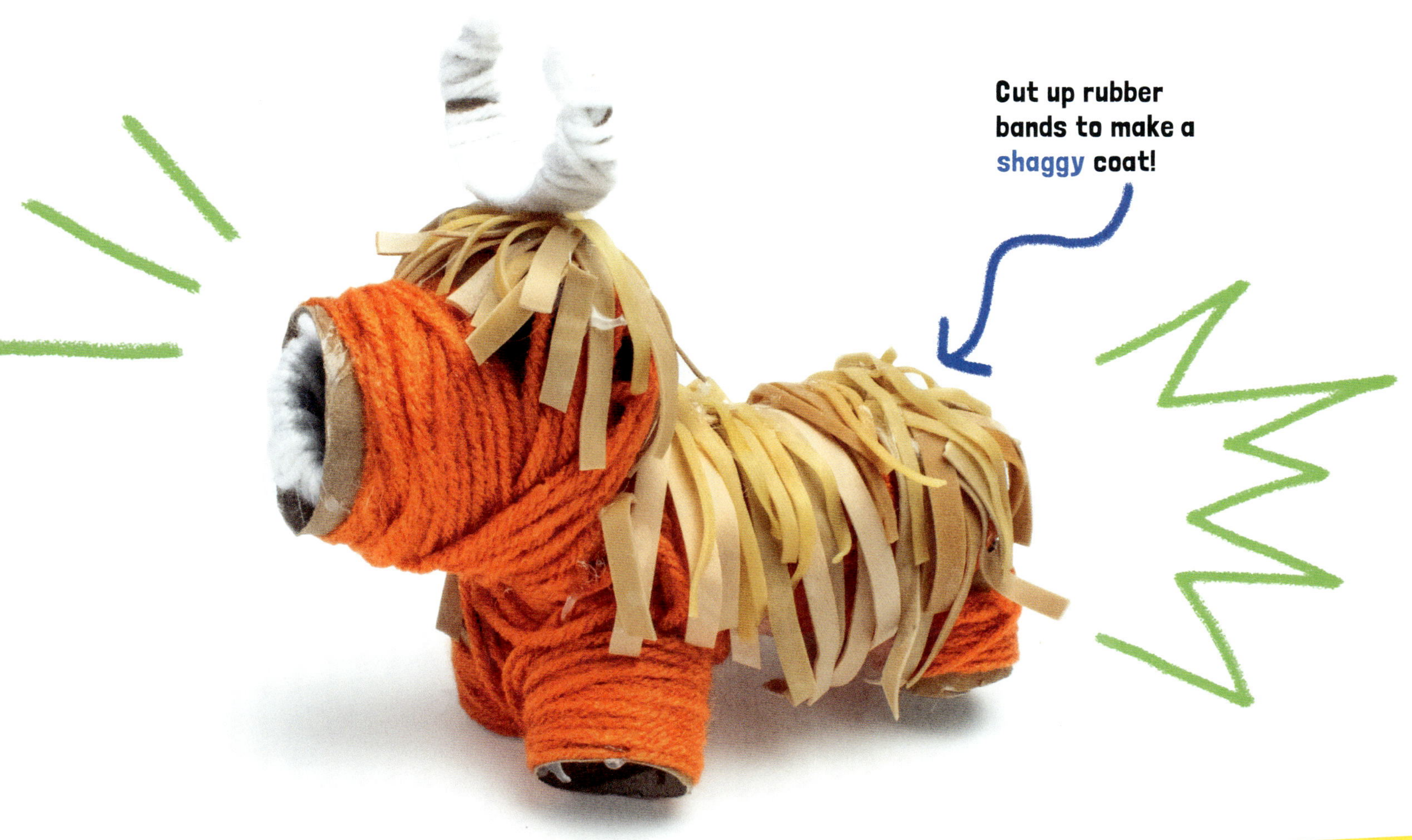

Your Turn!

How might you make a wind chime using paper tubes?

Could you weave rubber band pieces together to make a trivet?

How could you turn a ball of yarn into a cuddly critter?

PLAY WITH IT

Looking for something fun to do? Use paper tubes, rubber bands, and yarn to create your own toys and games!

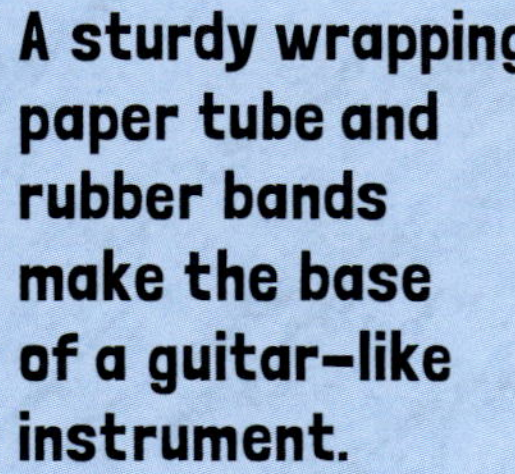

A sturdy wrapping paper tube and rubber bands make the base of a guitar-like instrument.

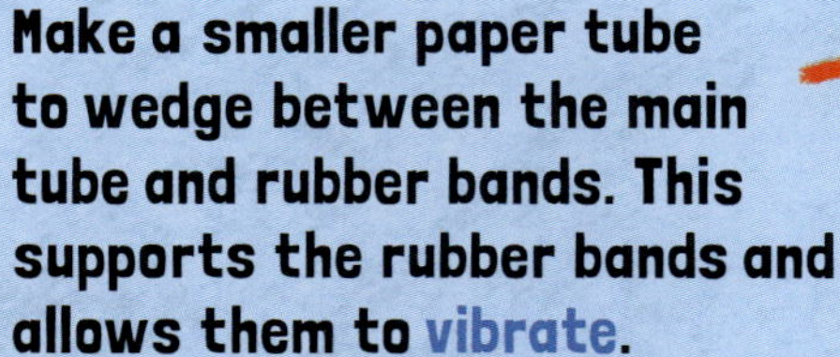

Make a smaller paper tube to wedge between the main tube and rubber bands. This supports the rubber bands and allows them to vibrate.

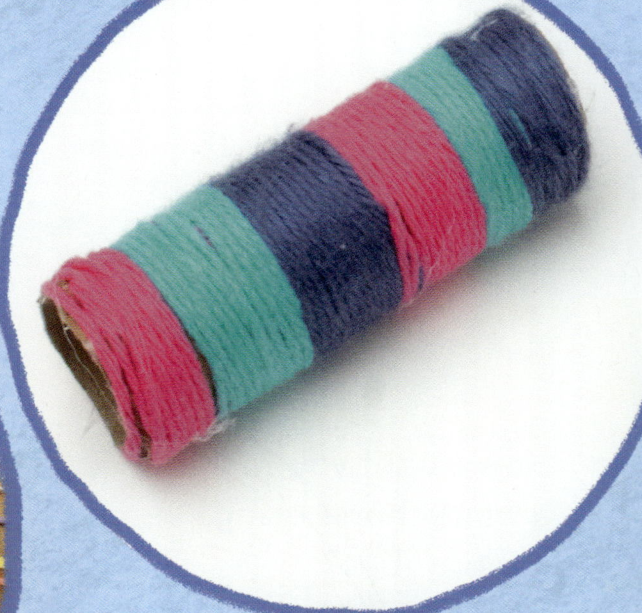

Wrap the ends of the tube in yarn to keep the strings in place.

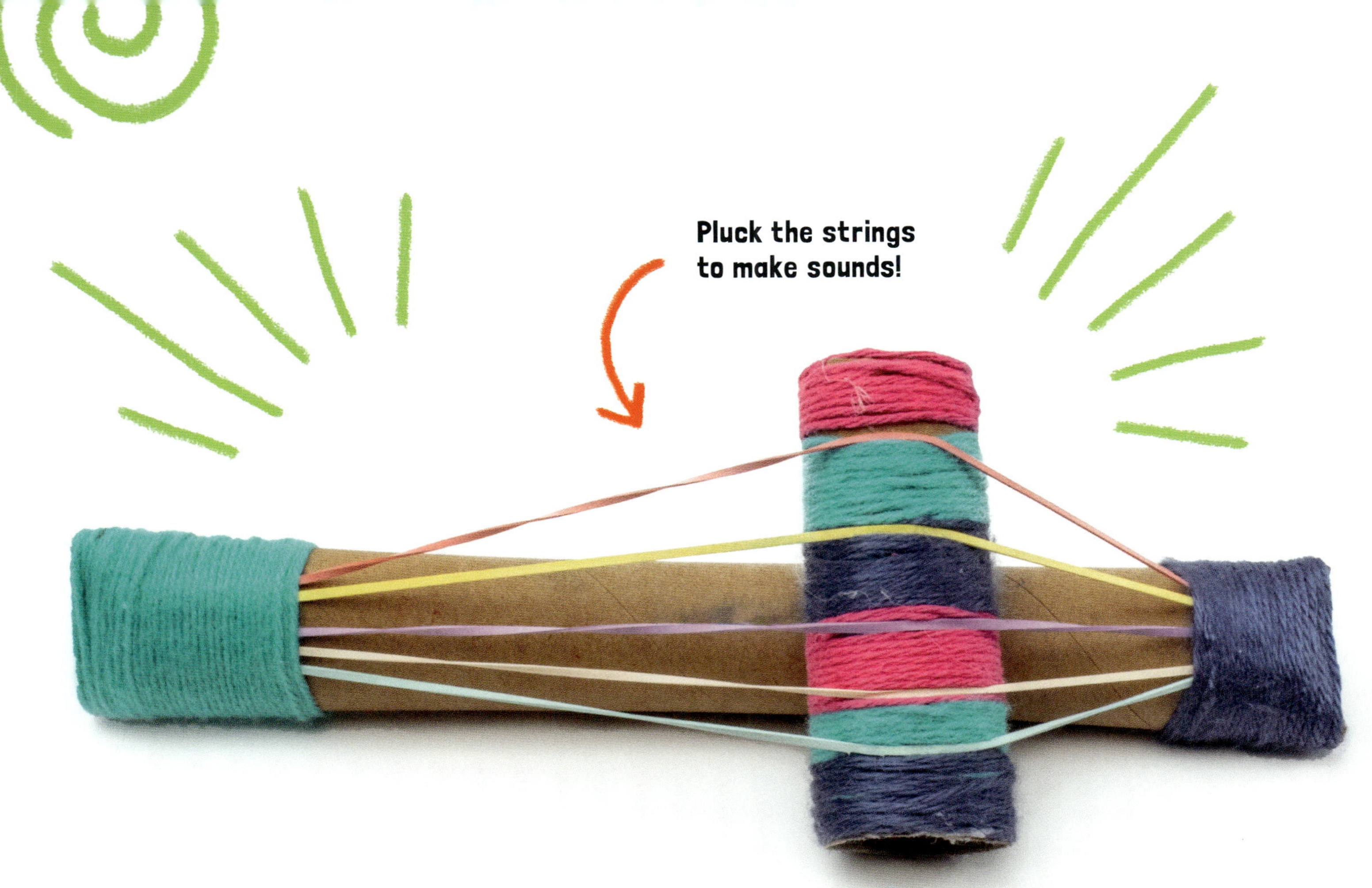

Your Turn!

Could you make a paper tube track for a marble?

How would you create a **catapult** out of rubber bands?

Could you make tiny toy figures out of yarn?

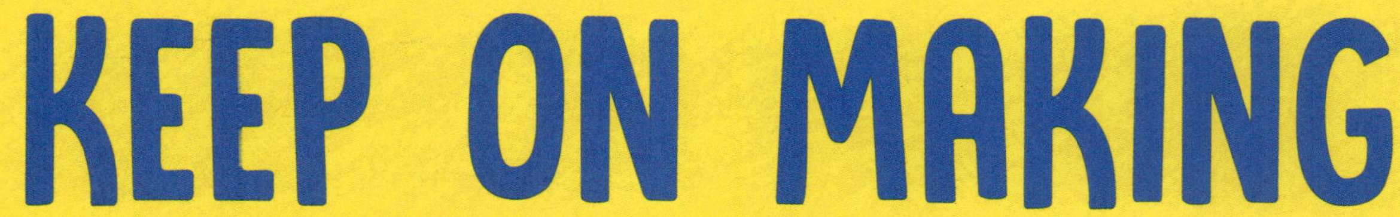

KEEP ON MAKING

Your paper tube, rubber band, and yarn projects may look complete, but don't close your makerspace toolbox yet. Think about what would make these projects even better. What would you do differently if you made each one again? What would happen if you used different methods or added another material?

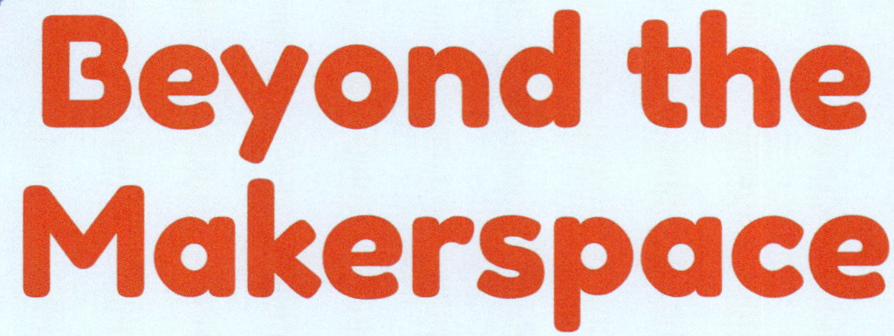

Beyond the Makerspace

You can use your makerspace toolbox beyond the makerspace! You might use it to accomplish everyday tasks, such as organizing your desk or decorating an old T-shirt. But makers use the same toolbox to do big things. One day, these tools could help treat sick people or forecast the weather. Turn your world into a makerspace! What problems could you solve?

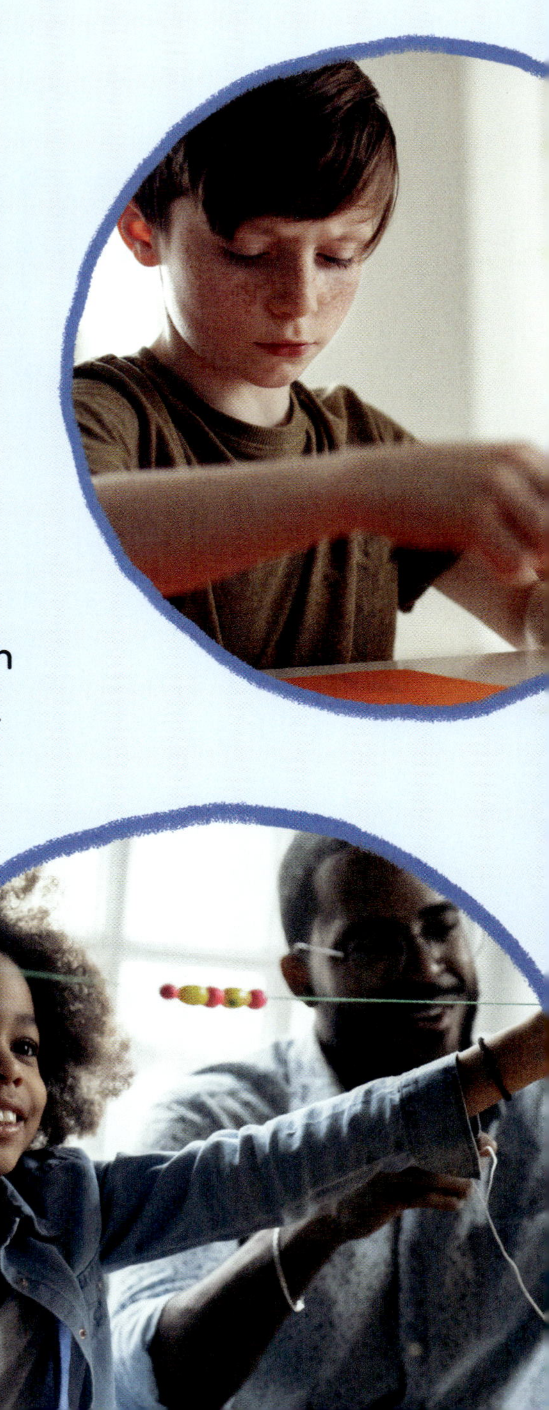

GLOSSARY

accessory – a piece of jewelry or clothing that makes an outfit appear more complete.

canvas – a piece of cloth or other material on which an artist paints.

catapult – a machine used to throw things.

collaboration – the act of working with others.

design – to plan how something will appear or work. A design is a sketch or outline of something that will be made.

detail – a small part of something.

flexible – easy to move or bend.

grid – a pattern with rows of squares, such as a checkerboard.

shaggy – made up of long, tangled hair or fur.

solution – an answer to, or a way to solve, a problem.

suspenders – straps worn over the shoulders that help hold up pants or a skirt.

3D – having three dimensions, such as length, width, and height.

trivet – a pad or stand on which hot pots or dishes are placed.

vibrate – to make very small, quick movements back and forth.